Water Babies
Seal Pups

by Ruth Owen

Consultant:
Dr. Edward H. Miller
Biology Department
Memorial University of Newfoundland

BEARPORT
PUBLISHING

New York, New York

Credits

Cover and Title Page, © Wayne Lynch/All Canada Photos/Superstock and © Bronwyn Photo/Shutterstock; 4–5, © Michio Hoshino/Minden Pictures/FLPA; 6, © Cosmographics; 7, © T. Walker/Photri Images/Alamy; 8–9, © Wayne Lynch/All Canada Photos/Alamy; 10–11, © FloridaStock/Shutterstock; 10, © Gabriela Staebler/Corbis Bridge/Alamy; 12, © Stone Nature Photography/Alamy; 13, © Image Plan/Corbis RF/Alamy; 15, © Michio Hoshino/Minden Pictures/FLPA; 17, © Keren Su/China Span/Alamy; 18–19, © S. Cook/IFAW, the International Fund for Animal Welfare; 20, © S. Cook/IFAW, the International Fund for Animal Welfare; 21, © Michio Hoshino/Minden Pictures/FLPA; 22T, © Cosmographics; 22B, © FloridaStock/Shutterstock; 23T, © Vladimir Melnik/Shutterstock; 23B, © Franco Banfi/seapics.com.

Publisher: Kenn Goin
Senior Editor: Lisa Wiseman
Creative Director: Spencer Brinker
Design: Emma Randall
Editor: Mark J Sachner
Photo Researcher: Ruby Tuesday Books Ltd

Library of Congress Cataloging-in-Publication Data

Owen, Ruth, 1967–
  Seal pups / by Ruth Owen.
     p. cm. — (Water babies)
  Includes bibliographical references and index.
  ISBN 978-1-61772-605-7 (library binding) — ISBN 1-61772-605-2 (library binding)
  1. Seals (Animals) —Infancy—Juvenile literature. I. Title.
  QL737.P63O94 2013
  599.79139—dc23
                                   2012017875

For more information, write to Bearport Publishing Company, Inc., 45 West 21st Street, Suite 3B, New York, New York 10010. Printed in the United States of America.

10 9 8 7 6 5 4 3 2 1

Contents

Meet a seal pup 4

Where do harp seals live? 6

All about harp seals 8

A newborn pup 10

A growing pup..................................... 12

Mom goes fishing 14

All alone 16

Time to go swimming 18

Growing up.. 20

Glossary...22

Index 24

Read more 24

Learn more online 24

About the author 24

Meet a seal pup

A fluffy, white harp seal **pup** wakes up next to her mother.

It is a freezing cold morning.

harp seal pup

The baby seal doesn't live in a warm home, though.

She lives outdoors, on the ice, in one of the coldest places on Earth.

harp seal mother

Where do harp seals live?

Harp seals live in cold oceans in a part of the world called the **Arctic**.

They can be found in cold waters inside the Arctic Circle.

They also live in the cold waters just outside the Arctic circle.

Asia

Arctic Ocean

Europe

Arctic Circle

Pacific Ocean

North America

Africa

Atlantic Ocean

N
W   E
S

South America

Where harp seals live

Adult seals spend most of their time swimming in the ocean.

Sometimes they rest on floating ice.

adult harp seal

All about harp seals

An adult harp seal has pale gray fur and a dark patch on its back.

The seal's fur keeps its body warm when it is not in water.

adult harp seal

pale gray fur

Under its fur, the seal has a thick layer of fat called **blubber**.

This fat keeps the seal warm in the cold ocean.

Adult harp seal size

A newborn pup

In spring, a female harp seal gives birth on the ice to just one pup.

The newborn pup has a fluffy coat of yellowish white fur to keep her warm.

yellowish white fur

newborn pup

After two or three days, the pup's fur turns bright white.

The pup is difficult to see against the white ice.

This keeps her hidden from polar bears that want to eat her.

pup with white fur

A growing pup

The seal pup drinks milk from her mother's body.

The milk is thick and full of fat.

mother seal

two-day-old pup drinking milk

The milk helps the seal pup's body make lots of blubber, which keeps her warm.

The pup grows bigger and heavier each day!

ten-day-old pup

Mom goes fishing

When the mother seal gets hungry, she hunts for fish and **shellfish**.

To find food, she looks for a crack in the ice and then dives into the ocean.

While she is hunting and eating underwater, the pup waits for her on the ice.

The mother seal can stay underwater for 15 minutes.

Then she pops back up to get some air and to check on her pup.

crack in ice

pup

mother seal

All alone

When the pup is about 12 days old, her mother goes to live on her own.

Soon, the pup's white fur starts to fall out and new silver-gray fur begins to grow.

The pup waits on the ice for her new coat to grow in completely.

It will take about three weeks.

During that time she has nothing to eat.

Time to go swimming

Once the pup has her new coat, she is ready to go swimming.

The pup finds a crack in the ice.

She slides into the water and starts to look for food.

Growing up

The five-week-old seal now spends her days in the ocean.

She hunts for fish and shellfish.

young seal with new coat

One day, in about five years, she will be ready to have a pup of her own!

newborn pup

mother seal

Glossary

Arctic (ARK-tic) the area inside the Arctic Circle; it is the northernmost area on Earth and includes the Arctic Ocean and North Pole

blubber (BLUH-bur) a layer of fat under the skin of animals, such as seals, whales, and polar bears

pup (PUP) the baby of an animal such as a seal or a sea otter

shellfish (SHEL-fish) sea creatures such as shrimp and crabs that live in water and have a hard, outer shell

Index

Arctic 6

blubber 9, 13

fish 14, 20

food 12–13, 14, 16, 18, 20

fur 8, 10–11, 16–17

hunting 14, 20

ice 7, 10–11, 14–15, 18

milk 12–13

ocean 6-7, 9, 14, 20

shellfish 14, 20

sizes 9, 13

swimming 7, 18

Read more

Kalman, Bobbie. *Seals and Sea Lions (The Living Ocean)*. New York: Crabtree (2006).

Lang, Aubrey. *Baby Seal (Nature Babies)*. Markham, Ontario: Fitzhenry & Whiteside (2002).

Martin-James, Kathleen. *Harp Seals (Early Bird Nature Books)*. Minneapolis: Lerner (2009).

Learn more online

To learn more about seals, visit
www.bearportpublishing.com/WaterBabies

About the author

Ruth Owen has been writing children's books for more than ten years. She particularly enjoys working on books about animals and the natural world. Ruth lives in Cornwall, England, just minutes from the ocean. She loves gardening and caring for her family of llamas.